SPIRITUAL WARFARE

by Brian Brodersen

THE WORD FOR TODAY
P.O. Box 8000, Costa Mesa, CA
92628

Spiritual Warfare
by Brian Brodersen
General Editor: Chuck Smith
Published by **The Word for Today**
P.O. Box 8000, Costa Mesa, CA 92628
(800) 272-WORD (9673)
http://www.twft.com

ISBN 0-936728-54-4

Table of Contents

Preface

When Luke wrote the message of the gospel to Theophilus, he declared that his desire was to set forth in order a declaration of those things that are most surely believed among us. Luke desired that Theophilus might know the certainty of those things in which he had been instructed.

We seem to be living in a day of spiritual confusion. Paul wrote to the Ephesians that they not be as children, tossed to and fro with every wind of doctrine by the slight of men and the cunning craftiness whereby they lie in wait to deceive. Because of all the confusion in the church today, and the many winds of doctrine that continue to blow through the body of Christ, we felt that it would be good to have various pastors write booklets that would address the issues and give to you the solid biblical basis of what we believe and why we believe it.

Our purpose is that the spiritual house that

you build will be set upon the solid foundation of the eternal Word of God, thus we know that it can withstand the fiercest storms.

Pastor Chuck Smith
Calvary Chapel of Costa Mesa, California

CHAPTER 1

SPIRITUAL WARFARE

Put on the whole armor of God, that you may be able to stand against the wiles of the devil. For we do not wrestle against flesh and blood, but against principalities, against powers, against the rulers of the darkness of this age, against spiritual hosts of wickedness in the heavenly places.

Ephesians 6:11–12

The Christian life is not simply believing in

Jesus and living happily ever after. It would be nice if that were the case. However anyone who has sought to seriously follow the Lord has found it to be otherwise. Jesus said to His followers that life in this world would be marked by tribulation and opposition. That opposition comes to us in a large degree from the devil and a multitude of wicked spirits who form a united front against the kingdom of God. Now I am certain that every Christian has experienced this opposition and some more acutely than others. I am also certain that many have not known that the source of the opposition was spiritual.

One of Satan's most effective strategies is to keep us ignorant of the existence of this warfare, to disguise himself so well that we do not recognize what is actually taking place. As C.S. Lewis said in his preface to *The Screwtape Letters:* "The demons hail with delight the materialist who disbelieves their existence." Although Lewis' statement might not apply to any of us directly because we are Christians, not materialists, it does apply inasmuch as, although we are Christians, quite often we live in oblivion to the spiritual realm that surrounds us.

Our purpose in this study is to be introduced to the reality of spiritual warfare, and in doing so to be helped on our way to victory in this battle.

The Opposition

We begin with a consideration of the inspiration behind the conflict: the devil and his angels. Who is the devil? Is he a real entity or just a mythological figure? The Bible teaches that the devil is a real person, a spirit being who was originally God's most glorious creature, but, by an act of rebellion, has become God's arch enemy (Isaiah 14). The Bible tells us that he is incredibly powerful, exceedingly intelligent, and immeasurably evil. Scripture also teaches that he is perpetually at war with God and His people. He is the commander and chief of a multitude of creatures similar to himself. These creatures are referred to by Paul as *"principalities and powers, the rulers of the darkness of this world, spiritual wickedness in high places."* All of these indicate organized opposition.

By way of analogy, consider the Roman empire. Caesar sat in Rome and made policy based upon his counsel with the senate. The senators would pass the decisions of the Counsel down to the governors and rulers who would then implement their decisions. Likewise, within the kingdom of Satan there are those high ranking officials making policy and those lower ranks that implement the policy.

The tenth chapter of Daniel's prophecy gives us insight into the kingdom of Satan.

> *In the third year of Cyrus king of Persia, a revelation was given to Daniel (who was called Belteshazzar). Its message was true and it concerned a great war. The understanding of the message came to him in a vision.*
>
> *At that time I, Daniel, mourned for three weeks. I ate no choice food; no meat or wine touched my lips; and I used no lotions at all until the three weeks were over.*
>
> *On the twenty-fourth day of the first month, as I was standing on the bank of the great river, the Tigris, I looked up and there before me was a man dressed in linen, with a belt of the finest gold around his waist. His body was like chrysolite, his face like lightning, his eyes like flaming torches, his arms and legs like the gleam of burnished bronze, and his voice like the sound of a multitude.*
>
> *I, Daniel, was the only one who saw the vision; the men with me did not see it, but such terror overwhelmed them that they fled and hid them-*

> *selves. So I was left alone, gazing at this great vision; I had no strength left, my face turned deathly pale and I was helpless. Then I heard him speaking, and as I listened to him, I fell into a deep sleep, my face to the ground.*
>
> *A hand touched me and set me trembling on my hands and knees. He said, "Daniel, you who are highly esteemed, consider carefully the words I am about to speak to you, and stand up, for I have now been sent to you." And when he said this to me, I stood up trembling.*
>
> *Then he continued, "Do not be afraid, Daniel. Since the first day that you set your mind to gain understanding and to humble yourself before your God, your words were heard, and I have come in response to them."*
>
> ***"But the prince of the Persian kingdom resisted me twenty-one days.** Then Michael, one of the chief princes, came to help me, because I was detained there with the king of Persia."*
>
> *"Now I have come to explain to you what will happen to your people in the future, for the vision concerns a time yet to come."*
>
> Daniel 10:1–14 (NIV)

Notice what the angel said: *"the prince of the Persian kingdom resisted me twenty-one days."*

Cyrus was the king of Persia at that time, yet, he most certainly was not the one resisting this angelic messenger. The reference is to the spiritual power behind the Persian Empire. A similar thing is said in Isaiah 14 and Ezekiel 28 where the prophets are prophesying against the kings of Babylon and Tyre. As they are prophesying, they suddenly and without explanation begin to address the spiritual power behind these earthly rulers. Therefore, we must also realize that the world we live in is not what it appears to be (essentially material), it also has a spiritual dimension and is actually governed by *"wicked spirits in high places."* It is imperative that we recognize this biblical truth.

Let me cite one more example of this invisible kingdom from the New Testament. Do you remember when the Lord was being tempted? Satan showed Him all the kingdoms of the world and their glory and said to Him, *"All this authority I will give You, and their glory; for this has been delivered to me, and I give it to whomever I wish"* (Luke 4:6). Jesus did not dispute Satan's claim of authority over the kingdoms of the world nor his ability to give them to whomever he wished. As a matter of fact, Jesus affirmed Satan's claim when He later referred to him as *"the ruler of this world"* (John 14:30). These are biblical facts which we need to understand. I believe many Christians have been seduced into thinking the way that the secular person thinks, looking at everything as merely related to man and natural processes. However, Paul says, *"we wrestle not against flesh and blood."* The conflict is ultimately with these spirit forces and unless we understand this we are defeated from the very onset.

The Conflict

The next thing we need to consider is the intimate nature of the conflict indicated by the term "wrestle." There are really two aspects to this spiritual warfare. There is the general aspect in which the collective forces of God are battling the collective forces of Satan. Then there is also a very personal aspect where you and I are engaged in hand to hand combat with demonic spirits. It's a wrestling match. It's intimate. It's personal. It's deadly. As a Christian you are being studied, stalked, and assaulted regularly. Failure to realize this can result in your becoming a casualty in this conflict. Maybe at this point you're saying, "Wait a minute; aren't you going a bit overboard with this? What do you mean I'm being studied, stalked, and assaulted by demons? This sounds fanatical."

I can assure you that I'm not being fanatical, but rather, scriptural. I'm simply stating what the Bible teaches generally and referring specifically to what is recorded in the case of Job.

> *One day the angels came to present themselves before the LORD, and Satan also came with them. The LORD said to Satan, "Where have you come from?" Satan answered the Lord, "From roaming through the earth and going back and forth in it."*
>
> *Then the LORD said to Satan, "Have you considered my servant Job? There is no one on earth like him; he is blameless and upright, a man who fears God and shuns evil." "Does Job fear God for nothing?" Satan replied. "Have you not put a hedge around him and his household and everything he has?" (NIV)*

You see, Satan had studied Job. He had stalked him. Very shortly he would assault him. Satan's tactics have not changed over the centuries. Today we are subject to the same kind of attacks Job experienced. I hope I'm not creating paranoia in anyone, that surely isn't my intention. My intention is to help you to see and understand the world and your own personal experiences through a biblical lens. Christians, today more than ever, need a biblical world view, which includes a belief in and understanding of the spiritual realm.

The Battle Is the Lord's

Now that we've established the reality of spiritual warfare we need to know how we are to survive in this invisible battle. The first thing to remember is that *"the battle is the Lord's,"* and therefore it is essential that we be *"strong in the Lord and in the power of His might"* (Ephesians 6:10). We have no natural power with which to contend with the forces of darkness. If I am to be victorious I must draw my strength from the Lord. It was this understanding that gave victory to men like David and Jehoshaphat.

When David faced Goliath he made it clear that he stood in God's strength:

> *Then David said to the Philistine, "You come to me with a sword, with a spear, and with a javelin. But I come to you in the name of the LORD of hosts, the God of the armies of Israel, whom you have defied. This day the LORD will deliver you into my hand, and I will strike you and take your head from you.... Then all this assembly will*

> *know that the Lord does not save with sword and spear; for the battle is the LORD's and He will give you into our hands."*
>
> 1 Samuel 17:45–47

Likewise when Jehoshaphat cried to the Lord for deliverance from his enemies, the prophet, Jehaziel, responded: *"Thus says the LORD to you: 'Do not be afraid nor dismayed because of this great multitude, for the battle is not yours, but God's'"* (2 Chronicles 20:15). It is critical that we remember this lest we be overcome with fear and discouragement.

The Weapons of Our Warfare

Another important point to remember is that; *"the weapons of our warfare are not carnal, but mighty in God"* (2 Corinthians 10:4,5). The word carnal is the antithesis of *spiritual* and refers to that which is merely human. Apart from the power of God, all of our energies combined are to no avail against the powers of darkness. Since we are in a spiritual battle we have need of spiritual weapons. That is exactly what God has supplied us with—*"weapons mighty in God for pulling down strongholds, casting down imaginations, and every high thing that exalts itself against the knowl-*

edge of God...." Weapons mighty in God! The word "mighty" could be translated "dynamically powerful." God has supplied us with more than we need for victory. Our need is to tap into what's already available to us.

What are the "weapons" God has given to us? They are simply prayer, the Word of God, and worship. We must be thoroughly immersed in these if we are going to successfully fight the *"good fight of faith."* Later, we'll take an in-depth look at these "weapons that are mighty in God," but for now, we move on to a further consideration of the enemy.

Chapter 2

The God of This Age

Now there was a day when the sons of God came to present themselves before the LORD, and Satan also came among them.

And the LORD said to Satan, "From where do you come?" So Satan answered the LORD and said, "From going to and fro on the earth, and from walking back and forth on it."

Job 1:6–7

From this passage, found in the book of Job, we see that our enemy, Satan, is indeed alive and well on planet earth. Therefore the question is: What is he doing? The answer: a whole lot more than most people blame him for. Let's take a look at some of the devil's activity in the world.

The Natural Realm

The first thing we want to consider is the devil's activity in the realm of nature. The Bible teaches that the devil has a certain degree of power over nature. It is therefore my belief that many of those things that we would glibly refer to as "natural disasters" or "acts of God" are actually manifestations of Satan's work. Now, I'm not saying that every catastrophe is a result of satanic activity, but, when you consider the death and destruction that result from these things, and the subsequent blame that is generally placed upon God, I think it is valid to consider many of these events as satanically orchestrated. At the very least Satan uses "natural disasters" in an attempt to destroy, discourage, and defeat the work of God in the world. We do have a biblical basis for our thinking on this. We turn once again to the Book of Job:

Then the LORD said to Satan, "Have you considered My servant Job, that there is none like him on the earth, a blameless and upright man, one who fears God and shuns evil?"

So Satan answered the LORD and said, "Does Job fear God for nothing?

"Have You not made a hedge around him, around his household, and around all that he has on every side? You have blessed the work of his hands, and his possessions have increased in the land.

"But now, stretch out Your hand and touch all that he has, and he will surely curse You to Your face!"

So the LORD said to Satan, "Behold, all that he has is in your power; only do not lay a hand on his person." So Satan went out from the presence of the LORD.

Now there was a day when his sons and daughters were eating and drinking wine in their oldest brother's house; and a messenger came to Job and said, "The oxen were plowing and the donkeys feeding beside them, when the Sabeans raided them and took them away—indeed they have killed the servants with the edge of the sword; and I alone have escaped to tell you!"

While he was still speaking, another also came

> *and said, "The fire of God fell from heaven and burned up the sheep and the servants, and consumed them; and I alone have escaped to tell you!"*
>
> *While he was still speaking, another also came and said, "The Chaldeans formed three bands, raided the camels and took them away, yes, and killed the servants with the edge of the sword; and I alone have escaped to tell you!"*
>
> *While he was still speaking, another also came and said, "Your sons and daughters were eating and drinking wine in their oldest brother's house, and suddenly a great wind came from across the wilderness and struck the four corners of the house, and it fell on the young people, and they are dead; and I alone have escaped to tell you!"*
>
> Job 1:8–19 (NIV)

Here is a classic example of what I'm talking about. The fire that fell from the sky and destroyed the flocks and the servants, and the wind that caused the house to collapse on Job's children killing them were a direct result of the devil's activity. Yet the messenger referred to the fire as ***"The Fire of God."*** Satan destroys lives and then seeks to put the blame on God. This is still true today. Think about the response of so many to the recent earthquakes, fires, floods, and storms that have devastated parts of the United States. As we listen to the victims being interviewed on television or read their statements in the newspaper, we find constant references to God, most of them negative and somehow implying God is to blame. But this is a part of the devil's activity.

As a matter of fact, the name "devil" means slanderer or accuser. Satan stirs up the forces of nature bringing death and destruction and then accuses God of being responsible for the whole mess. The tragedy is that most people believe him. Someone might ask at this point; are you saying that earthquakes, floods, and hurricanes, etc. are the work of Satan? My answer to that is: not always, but perhaps more often than we think. When you consider Satan's goals (i.e., to kill and destroy), "natural disasters" provide for him an excellent arena in which to work.

Human Affairs

But it doesn't stop there! Satan is also busy at work in the affairs of men. Whether it's international politics, the media, academia, the entertainment industry, or the fads and fashions of the world, his influence is felt. Paul referred to Satan as *"the prince of the power of the air, the spirit that now works in the children of disobedience"* (Ephesians 2:2). From evolutionary theory to Marxist philosophy, from racial prejudice to multi-culturalism, from gang violence to world wars, from the sexual revolution to AIDS, from broken homes to the violent crime epidemic, from alcoholism to drug addiction, Satan's work is evident. The hatred and violence, the death and destruction, the pain and the misery, from the beginning of history until today are all to a large degree due to the activity of the devil. Truly as the Apostle John said *"the whole world lies under the sway of the wicked one"* (1 John 5:19).

False Religion

Another manifestation of the devil's activity is false religion. This is Satan's masterpiece and perhaps his greatest means of influence. It is also his most deadly weapon because it is aimed directly at men's souls. The ultimate goal of the devil is to keep a human soul from the salvation that is in Christ, and he will do anything in his power, even encourage religious devotion, to obtain the desired results. What do I mean by "false religion"? Everything from Hinduism, with its myriad of gods, to Islam, and its one unknowable god, Allah. Also included would be the pseudo-Christian cults (i.e., Jehovah's Witnesses, Mormons, Christian Science, etc.). These are all part of the devil's activity in the world. The Apostle Paul said: *"For Satan himself transforms himself into an angel of light"* (2 Corinthians 11:14). Through these false religious systems Satan has kept multitudes of people blinded to the truth, as Paul also said:"... *if our gospel is veiled, it is veiled to those who are perishing, whose minds the god of this age has blinded, who do not believe, lest the light of the gospel of the glory of Christ, who is the image of God, should shine on them"* (2 Corinthians 4:4).

As we come to a greater awareness of Satan's activity in the world, may it lead us to a greater use of the mighty weapons of prayer and proclamation of the gospel. It's through prayer that catastrophe can be turned into an opportunity for God to work. It's through prayer and proclamation of the gospel that God intervenes in the affairs of men by pouring out His Spirit and bringing about radical change. The Reformation and the Great Awakenings are good examples of God using adverse conditions to bring about His work. It's through the proclamation of the gospel that men are freed from the blinding effects of false religion and brought to a saving knowledge of Christ.

Any good military strategist makes it a point to know the workings of his enemy, the more familiar we are with the devil's activity the more effective we will be in overcoming him and helping others to do so. We proceed now to still another aspect of the devil's activity, "The wiles of the devil."

Chapter 3

The Wiles of the Devil

Put on the whole armor of God, that you may be able to stand against the wiles of the devil... above all, taking the shield of faith with which you will be able to quench all the fiery darts of the wicked one."

Ephesians 6:11–12,16

The "wiles of the devil" and the "fiery darts of the wicked one" although covering a broad range of activity are no doubt inclusive of Satan's attack upon our mind and emotions. These attacks result in such experiences as condemnation, doubt, fear, evil thoughts, and depression. Now, I do not claim to understand how it is that Satan or demons can access our minds and emotions, but that they can is clear both from Scripture, and the testimony of many of God's servants throughout the long history of the church. Take for example what is recorded in 1 Chronicles 21:1, *"Now Satan stood up against Israel, and* ***moved*** *David to number Israel."* When David was suddenly impressed to number the people, I doubt that he was aware that he was being influenced by Satan, yet that is exactly what happened.

When we come to the New Testament we find a similar instance with the Apostle Peter recorded in Matthew 16:13–23. There Jesus asked the disciples, *"who do you say that I am?"* Simon Peter answered and said, *"You are the Christ, the Son of the Living God."*

Then, as Jesus proceeded to tell them about His coming rejection by the leaders at Jerusalem, and His subsequent execution, Peter, well-meaning but misguided, took Jesus aside and began to rebuke Him saying, *"Far be it from You, Lord; this shall not happen to You!"*

The response of Jesus to Peter illustrates my point. Jesus turned and said to Peter, *"Get behind Me, Satan! You are an offense to Me, for you are not* ***mindful*** *of the things of God, but the things of men."* Peter was mentally under the influence of Satan; his thoughts at this point were satanically inspired. Peter's response and the subsequent rebuke of Christ is all the more remarkable in that we are told that his earlier confession was a matter of divine revelation.

Perhaps the most tragic example of Satan's attack upon the mind and emotions is found in John 13:2 where we read; *"the devil* ***put it into the heart*** *of Judas Iscariot to betray Jesus."*

In each of these cases, we see the enemy's ability to influence the way we think and feel. Having established that fact, we now want to take a closer look at some of the "wiles of the devil" in order to become aware of and avoid being ensnared by them.

Condemnation

A common tactic of the devil is to make you feel cut off from God's love and forgiveness. This occurs most often after some failure on your part. Maybe you did something that you knew you shouldn't have done or you didn't do something that you knew you should have. It's then that condemnation usually strikes. However, it is important to distinguish between conviction and condemnation. Conviction is a legitimate work of the Holy Spirit that produces guilt over our sins and then leads us to the cross to receive forgiveness. Condemnation, on the other hand, produces guilt and leaves the victim with a sense of hopelessness.

The devil moves in and begins to suggest to you that God is finished with you; he will say, "You've gone too far this time." He implies that forgiveness is unavailable to you. You might even have overwhelming feelings that God has abandoned you and that He no longer loves you. All of this is typical of the *"fiery darts of the wicked one."* The fiery darts of the enemy can only be overcome by taking up the shield of faith, faith in the Word of God. The power of condemnation lies in Satan's ability to deceive us into thinking that God is the one condemning us. For after all, if God is against us, who can be for us? However, this is the exact opposite of what is true! In Romans 8:1 Paul says; *"There is therefore now no condemnation to those who are in Christ Jesus..."* And then in verse 31 he says; *"...God is for us, who can be against us?"* In verses 33–34 he asks; *"Who shall bring a charge against God's elect? It is God who justifies. Who is he who condemns? It is Christ who died, and furthermore is also risen, who is even at the right hand of God, who also makes intercession for us."* Those accusing thoughts, those condemning feelings come from the *"accuser of the brethren."* It is only by confidence in the blood of the Lamb that we can overcome satanic condemnation.

If you've sinned, don't let the devil drive you away from the Lord through condemnation. Instead, confess your sin and remember that *"He is faithful and just to forgive your sins and to cleanse you from all unrighteousness"* (1 John 1:9).

Doubt

Another of the devil's darts, is to plant doubt in our minds. Satan will try to get you to doubt everything from God's existence to your salvation. He is especially concerned with casting doubt on the Word of God. An important thing to remember on this subject is that there is a difference between the temptation to doubt and the sin of unbelief. It's possible to be plagued by doubt and yet innocent of the sin of unbelief.

The great English preacher Charles Spurgeon was very familiar with this particular form of temptation. He said, "My peculiar temptation has been constant unbelief. I know that God's promise is true. Yet does this temptation incessantly assail me—doubt Him, distrust Him, etc." Spurgeon, of course, resisted the temptation, but his statements indicate that he struggled constantly in this area.

So once again, I remind you it is not sin when you are oppressed by the temptation to doubt. Doubt only becomes sin when we act upon it and allow it to control us. Satan tempted Eve to doubt God's word. However, it wasn't until she submitted to his suggestions that she sinned. Just because you're tempted to doubt doesn't mean that you've sinned. You can refuse to give in to those suggestions.

When I was a young Christian, I had heard that certain scholars and theologians questioned the validity of some of the books of the Bible. At that point, Satan sought to plant doubt in my mind concerning the Word of God. The thought went something like this: "These men are theologians and have studied the Bible for years.

They know the Hebrew and the Greek. I know nothing. How could I possibly think I'm right and they're wrong?" Does that sound familiar? Or maybe you've had an experience like this: You are reading your Bible when suddenly your mind is flooded with questions like; "Are you sure Jesus Christ even existed? Could those miracles really have happened? How could someone rise from the dead? What about all the other religions? Isn't it a bit arrogant to think that Jesus is the only way to God?" And the list goes on and on.

Those are the kinds of things that Satan will suggest to you. He's always trying to undermine the Word of God. He tried it with Eve in the garden, "Has God really said...?" (Genesis 3:1). He tried it with Jesus in the wilderness, "If You are the Son of God...?" (Luke 4:3). You can be sure he'll try it with you. The Word of God is both our compass and rudder to guide us through this stormy Christian life. If the devil can get us to doubt just the smallest thing he can get us off course. If he can get us to doubt greater things we can end up shipwrecked. That is, of course, his goal. Don't give in to doubt. Recognize it as one of the devil's tactics and stand firm on the Word of God.

One last thing, don't confuse honest questions with doubt. Consider the difference between Zacharias' response to the angel Gabriel with Mary's response (Luke 1:18,34). Both seemingly asked the same question, "How shall this be?" It was not the question "how" but rather the attitude with which the question was posed. Zacharias asked in unbelief as if to say, "You've got to be kidding. No way!" Mary, on the other hand was asking in what manner God would accomplish such a wonder. This is evidenced in her final statement to Gabriel: "Behold the handmaiden of the Lord! Let it be to me according to your word." Mary was not doubting God's Word, she was submitting to His plan.

It's all right to ask questions. It's through asking questions that we learn. Through honest questions you can turn your temptations to doubt into opportunities to grow in your understanding of the Lord, His Word and His ways. At the end of every honest question you will find that God is true even as Paul concludes in Romans 3:4, *"Let God be true and every man a liar."*

Fear

Another of the devil's wiles is the use of fear tactics. He threatens evil consequences upon those who would trust and obey the Lord. When the 18th Century revivalist George Whitefield called upon his friend John Wesley to take over his open-air preaching ministry, John was suddenly struck with the impression that if he were to do so, he would die. Having sought divine guidance by randomly opening his Bible on four different occasions, the Scriptures seemed to confirm his fear of death. His fears proved to be nothing more than the work of the devil seeking to prevent him from entering into the work that God had called him to. It was actually through the acceptance of that invitation that John Wesley entered his evangelistic career which lasted more than fifty years and resulted in the conversion of tens of thousands and the forming of the Methodist Church.

A second example of this fear tactic is seen in the story of a Rabbi who through various circumstances came to believe that Jesus is the Messiah of Israel. When he received Christ he realized that he needed to choose a day on which to make a public confession of his faith by being baptized. His story of the events that transpired on the day of his baptism amply illustrate the devil's attempts to hinder God's work in us through this fear tactic. He said,

"Early that morning, about day break, I awakened with a shiver and it seemed as if someone spoke saying, 'What are you doing today?'"

"I sprang out of bed and walked up and down the room like one suffering from high fever almost not knowing what I was doing. I had been anxiously waiting to be baptized as I was looking forward with joy to the time when I could publicly confess the Lord Jesus Christ before men. But now a sudden change came over me. The voice that was talking to me was that of the great enemy of mankind, though of course he was so sly that I could not perceive at the time that it was Satan."

"Many questions were proposed to me rapidly one after another and perplexed me so that I felt ill mentally and physically. He questioned thus: 'you are going to be baptized aren't you? Do you know that as soon as you take this step you will be cut off from your wife whom you love so dearly? She can never live with you again. Do you realize that your four children who you are so fond of will never call you Papa or look in your face again? Your brothers, sisters and all your relatives will consider you dead and all their hearts will be broken forever. How can you be so cruel to your own flesh and blood? Your own people will despise and hate you more than ever before. You are cutting yourself off from your people. You have no friends in this world. You will be left alone to drift like a piece of timber on the ocean. What will become of your name, your reputation, your official position.'"

"These thoughts put to me in the form of the most audible questions by Satan whom I for the first time met as a personal enemy, distressed and almost unbalanced my mind. I could not sleep, neither could I eat. My friend who was with me, noticing this, tried to strengthen and encourage me in every way possible, but nothing availed. I knelt down in prayer to God but the satanic delusion was as strong as before."

He continues his story by describing what eventually took place. Feeling mentally and physically sick he went to inform the pastor that he would not be able to be baptized. About that same time another pastor along with his congregation felt impressed to pray for this man, knowing he was to be baptized that day. As they began to pray, suddenly the oppression lifted and instead of canceling out of his baptismal appointment he was baptized and made his public confession of Christ just as he had desired to do.

This man went on to become a powerful witness for the Lord forming what became known as the American Board of Missions to the Jews. He led many of his fellow Israelites to faith in the Messiah Jesus.

Did you notice how the devil threatened evil consequences if he were to obey the Lord? Yet this was nothing more than an idle threat just as it was with John Wesley. Satan will threaten you just as Saul threatened David or Tobiah and Sanballet threatened Nehemiah. But that is all he is able to do because *"Greater is He who is in you, than he who is in the world"* (1 John 4:4). Again, *"If God be for us who can be against us?"* (Romans 8:31). Don't let the enemy keep you out of the will of God through this fear tactic. Remember, *"God has not given us a spirit of fear, but of power, love, and a sound mind"* (2 Tim. 1:7). Our heavenly Father has our eternal best in mind. So yield to Him without fear. Watch what He will do. Father knows best.

Evil Thoughts and Imaginations

Another manifestation of the "wiles of the devil"

is evil thoughts. Have you ever been in prayer and had your mind suddenly assaulted by blasphemous thoughts? Have you ever been worshipping and had pornographic images flash across your mind? Have you ever gone through a period of time in which your mind was obsessed by deplorable thoughts, thoughts that sickened and oppressed you, thoughts that you longed to be delivered from, thoughts of sexual immorality, murder, or suicide? If so, you are not alone.

You know first hand what the Apostle Paul was referring to when he spoke of the "fiery darts" or more literally the flaming arrows of the wicked one. Now an important question to ask at this point is: How can I tell the difference between the flaming arrows of the wicked one and the sin of evil surmising? Evil surmising originates from within, as Jesus said: *"Out of the heart proceed evil thoughts..."* (Matthew 15:19). Evil surmising is within your power to control and has an element of delight in it. The flaming arrows of the wicked one, on the other hand, come from outside of you and are to a certain degree beyond your power to control. They are also offensive to you. You not only do not want to think these thoughts, you consciously reject them.

An experience from the life of Charles Spurgeon serves as an illustration. Having gone through a prolonged period of blasphemous assault upon his mind and being near the point of despair, he was now questioning even his salvation (For after all, how could a true Christian think such thoughts?). He finally confided in his grandfather who also happened to be a minister of the gospel. His grandfather asked him one simple question: "Do you take pleasure in those thoughts?" Young Spurgeon replied: "No, I hate them!" His grandfather responded, "Then have nothing to do with them. Do not own them because they are not yours, but the devil's."

The devil is subtle; he plants a thought in your mind and wants to make you think it's your thought. But don't own it; instead reject it and realize who's behind it. You can even turn the enemy's weapons back upon him by using those occasions as an opportunity for prayer and worship. You can be like Benaiah who *"wrested the spear out of the enemy's hand, and killed him with his own spear"* (2 Samuel 23:21).

> *Finally, brethren, whatever things are true, whatever things are noble, whatever things are just, whatever things are pure, whatever things are lovely, whatever things are of good report, if*

there is any virtue and if there is anything praise-worthy—meditate on these things.

Philippians 4:8

As nature abhors a vacuum, so our minds cannot long remain empty. Good thoughts leave no room for bad thoughts.

Depression

Depression is perhaps the most devastating of the "wiles of the devil" inasmuch as the devil gathers up all of the things we've discussed (condemnation, doubt, fear, evil thoughts and imaginations), wraps them in despair and leaves you with an overwhelming sense of hopelessness.

Many of God's people throughout the ages have known firsthand what it is to be depressed. You might be surprised to find that both the Psalmist and the Apostle Paul experienced depression. Listen to their words:

In the day of my trouble I sought the Lord; my hand was stretched out in the night without ceasing; my soul refused to be comforted.

I remembered God, and was troubled; I complained, and my spirit was overwhelmed.

> *You hold my eyelids open; I am so troubled that I cannot speak.*
>
> Psalm 77:2–4

> *...We were burdened beyond measure, above strength, so that we despaired even of life.*
>
> 2 Corinthians 1:8

We also have many examples from church history of those who suffered from depression. William Cowper, the great English poet and hymn writer, battled his entire life with manic-depression.

Charles Spurgeon said, "I, of all men, am perhaps the subject of the deepest depression at times... Depression so fearful I hope none of you ever get to such extremes of wretchedness as I go to."

So we see that God's people are not exempt from depression. Everyone suffers from depression from time to time, some more frequently and more severely than others. The question is then: How do we deal with depression?

First of all, we need to know what's causing it. There are basically four types of depression. There is depression that is organic in nature (a bodily malfunction, i.e., hormonal or chemical imbalances). Then there is circumstantial depression; the problems of life have gotten you down. Some depression is directly related to sin. And finally, there is depression that is the direct result of satanic activity.

How to know just what type of depression a person is dealing with is not always easy; however, God has promised wisdom for those who ask Him for it (James 1:5).

Once we discern the cause, we can proceed with the treatment. If the cause is organic, the treatment will be primarily medical. If the cause is circumstantial, the treatment will be getting a biblical perspective on your circumstances and trusting God. If the cause is sin, repentance is necessary. If the cause is satanic, the spiritual weapons of the Word of God and prayer are the only things that will avail.

Back in the days before there were antidepressants, William Cowper was prayed out of a deep, dark, suicidal depression by his faithful friend and pastor, John Newton. Although treatment with medications can be beneficial, these treatments should never be used to the exclusion of the Word of God and prayer. It is my opinion that regardless of the root cause of depression, there is a satanic aspect to it. Therefore, I believe that all depression regardless of its source, should be treated through biblical counseling and intense prayer.

If you have been plagued by depression, remember, *"the same sufferings are experienced by your brotherhood in the world... And God is faithful, who will not allow you to be tempted beyond what you are able, but with the temptation will also make the way of escape..."* (1 Peter 5:9 & 1 Corinthians 10:13). Don't believe the devil's lie that there's no hope, so you might as well just end it all now. Look to the Lord! Call upon His Name! Stand upon His Word! Pray, and ask others to pray for you. Seek godly counsel from a pastor or a mature Christian friend. Finally, know that *"the God of peace will crush Satan under your feet shortly"* (Romans 16:20).

We move now to consider one final aspect of the devil's war against us—temptation.

Chapter 4

Temptation

Be sober, be vigilant; because your adversary the devil walks about like a roaring lion, seeking whom he may devour.

Resist him, steadfast in the faith, knowing that the same sufferings are experienced by your brotherhood in the world.

1 Peter 5:8–9

Satan's most notorious activity is that of tempting mankind. Temptation is the solicitation to do evil, and is the common experience of all people, whether they are Christians or not. Yet, Satan puts forth extra effort in tempting Christians. He knows that if he can bring down a Christian he can to some degree discredit the church and bring reproach upon the name of the Lord. As David's sin with Bathsheba gave "great occasion to the enemies of the Lord to blaspheme" so it is with sinning Christians. This is one of Satan's motives for tempting believers. Another reason Satan will tempt you is simply because he hates you and wants to destroy you. He knows that *"sin, when it is full grown, brings forth death"* (James 1:15).

When Peter referred to Satan as *"a roaring lion, seeking whom he may devour"* (1 Peter 5:8), he was, no doubt, thinking of Satan's activity in tempting man. With death and destruction as the aim of the tempter we cannot afford to take temptation lightly. On the contrary, we must be sober and vigilant in dealing with our adversary, the devil.

Recognizing Temptation

The first thing we need to do, in relation to temptation, is to learn to recognize when we are being tempted.

One of Satan's attributes is subtlety. He disguises himself so well that quite often the one being tempted is oblivious to what is actually happening. Like the seasoned angler who knows just the right lure, Satan knows your areas of weakness and will tempt you accordingly. He can appear as an angel of light, a damsel in distress, as the solution to your financial problems or the answer to your poor self-image. The list goes on and on. Paul referred to this attribute of Satan when writing to the Corinthians. He said, *"I fear, lest somehow, as the serpent deceived Eve by his subtlety, so your minds may be corrupted from the simplicity that is in Christ"* (2 Corinthians 11:3).

Though temptation is sometimes difficult to recognize, you can be sure you're being tempted whenever you're faced with a situation that could lead you to rationalize, compromise, or in anyway disobey the Word of God.

Avoiding Temptation

Another important aspect in dealing with temptation is that you make every effort to avoid it. You can avoid temptation first of all by prayer. Jesus said, *"Watch and pray, lest you enter into temptation"* (Matthew 26:41). Secondly, you can avoid temptation by having a realistic view of yourself. This means recognizing your weaknesses and staying away from those things that pose a special problem for you. If you've had a problem with sexual sin, then you must do everything in your power to avoid any situation that could cause you to stumble. It might mean staying away from a certain person or group of people; it could mean avoiding certain forms of entertainment (i.e., the movie theater, and the TV—especially cable, or staying away from the magazine rack in the local convenience store).

If your problems have been alcohol or drug related then you need to avoid people, places, or situations that could lead you into temptation. This same principle applies in every area of weakness. If, after all of this, you still find yourself in a tempting situation, like that of Joseph, with Potiphar's wife, then the only recourse in such circumstances is to flee as Joseph did. Knowing your area of vulnerability is actually a step toward victory over temptation. Remember *"if any man thinks he stands, let him take heed lest he fall"* (1 Corinthians 10:12). Don't put yourself in a tempting situation, but rather, *"flee these things and pursue righteousness, godliness, faith, love... Fight the good fight of faith, lay hold on eternal life"* (1 Timothy 6:11–12).

Overcoming Temptation

The only good news about being tempted is that we can have the victory over temptation. It is crucial to know this. By listening to, or watching some Christians, you could get the impression that victory is an impossibility and that backsliding is just another facet of the Christian experience. Yet, nothing could be further from the truth. The Bible tells us that victory is possible. The Apostle John said: *"My little children, these things I write to you, so that you may not sin"* (1 John 2:1). James, in chapter 4, verses 7–8, instructs us on how to obtain the victory, *"Therefore submit to God. Resist the devil, and he will flee from you. Draw near to God and He will draw near to you."*

Victory begins with a total submission to God. If Jesus is not the Lord of our lives, it will be very difficult, if not impossible, to be victorious over temptation. Having submitted ourselves to God, we then resist the devil. Resisting the devil means we stand against him with the weapons that God has given to us. The primary weapon is the Word of God. As we resist, in due time, Satan will flee.

In Matthew 4:1–11 we see this beautifully illustrated in the life of Christ. Jesus, after fasting for forty days and forty nights, is met by Satan who says to Him, *"If You are the Son of God, command that these stones become bread."* Here our Lord does what we are instructed to do; He resists the devil. How? With the Word of God. *"It is written, man shall not live by bread alone, but by every word that proceeds from the mouth of God."*

Each time Satan came with a temptation, Jesus countered with the Word. We are to handle temptation exactly as Jesus did with the Word of God. When Satan tempts you to revert to your old habits, resist him with 2 Corinthians 5:17, *"If anyone is in Christ, he (or she) is a new creation; old things have passed away; behold, all things have become new."* And with Romans 6:11–12, *"Likewise you also, reckon yourselves to be dead indeed to sin, but alive to God in Christ Jesus our Lord. Therefore, do not let sin reign in your mortal body, that you should obey it in its lusts."*

When Satan tempts you with immorality or

substances that are forbidden by God, resist him with 1 Corinthians 6:19–20, *"Do you not know that your body is the temple of the Holy Spirit who is in you, whom you have from God, and you are not your own? For you were bought at a price; therefore glorify God in your body and in your spirit, which are God's."* It's in this practical consideration of temptation that we see the importance of David's statement: *"Your word have I hid in my heart that I might not sin against You"* (Psalm 119:11). Scripture memorization is a great asset when faced with temptation. Finally, remember *"that our old man was crucified with Him, that the body of sin might be done away with, that we should no longer be slaves of sin... and having been set free from sin, you became slaves of righteousness"* (Romans 6:6,18).

Having dealt with temptation we come to the end of this section of our study where we have concentrated primarily on the nature and activity of our adversary. From this point we will move on to a consideration of those things that will lead us to victory in this Christian warfare. Let me end this section with two very encouraging statements from the Word of God.

> *No temptation has overtaken you except such as is common to man; but God is faithful, who will*

not allow you to be tempted beyond what you are able, but with the temptation will also make the way of escape, that you may be able to bear it.

1 Corinthians 10:13

Seeing then that we have a great High Priest who has passed through the heavens, Jesus the Son of God, let us hold fast our confession.

For we do not have a High Priest who cannot sympathize with our weaknesses, but was in all points tempted as we are, yet without sin.

Let us therefore come boldly to the throne of grace, that we may obtain mercy and find grace to help in time of need.

Hebrews 4:14–16

Chapter 5

The Armor of God

Therefore take up the whole armor of God, that you may be able to withstand in the evil day, and having done all, to stand.

Stand therefore, having girded your waist with truth, having put on the breastplate of righteousness, and having shod your feet with the preparation of the gospel of peace; above all, taking the shield of faith with which you will be able to quench all the fiery darts of the wicked one.

And take the helmet of salvation, and the sword of the Spirit, which is the Word of God.

Ephesians 6:13–17

We now will consider the weapons of our warfare. In the passage above, Paul paints for us a picture of a Roman soldier fully dressed for battle and then explains that in a similar manner we are to take up the whole armor of God. He then lists for us the various pieces that make up the whole armor, using the Roman soldier as an analogy. Rather than getting preoccupied with the type of armor that was used by the Romans at that time, we want to simply get to the message behind the analogy. What is the point the apostle is wanting to make? What exactly is the armor of God?

The whole armor of God is essentially an understanding and application of the Word of God, the Scriptures. Each piece of the armor represents a different aspect of the truth and leads ultimately to a thorough understanding of and an ability to apply God's Word as a mighty force against the powers of darkness. Now, as we consider this armor, the majority of it is defensive. The armor is given to us to protect us from the attacks of the enemy. The belt of truth, the breastplate of righteousness, the boots of peace, the shield of faith, and the helmet of salvation are all for the most part defensive and enable us to stand without losing ground. This defensive aspect of the armor represents a detailed knowledge of the Word of God, and the great doctrines of the Christian faith contained therein.

Belt of Truth

The belt is mentioned first because it is the foundational piece of the armor. It gave the soldier mobility and strength. It is the belt of truth. The truths of the Word of God are the foundation from which this warfare is waged. To be girded with the truth means to have knowledge of and belief in the truth. The enemy cannot be withstood by human reason, tradition, speculative conviction, or by anything other than the truth of God's Word. Therefore, we must be prepared with it. Preparation with the Word of God comes by being immersed in the Word of God.

Breastplate of Righteousness

Next, we come to the breastplate of righteousness. The breastplate, of course, protected the vital organs—the heart, the lungs, the pancreas, the liver, etc. The ancients believed this part of the body to be the seat of the emotions. So, we speak of sorrow as being "broken-hearted" or use the term "bowels of mercy" as a way of describing compassion. Therefore, the breastplate is to protect us in the realm of our emotions. Notice, it is the breastplate of righteousness. Satan quite often attacks our emotions in regard to righteousness.

We've already talked about condemnation; the feeling that God is against us. When condemnation would overwhelm us, it's an understanding of the doctrine of the imputed righteousness of Christ that serves as our first line of defense. That knowledge is obtained through the Scriptures, *"For He made Him who knew no sin to be sin for us, that we might become the righteousness of God in Him"* (2 Corinthians 5:21). *"He made us accepted in the Beloved"* (Ephesians 1:6). *"That I may be found in Him, not having my own righteousness... but that which is through faith in Christ, the righteousness which is from God by faith"* (Phil. 3:9). Christ's imputed righteousness is what Paul was primarily referring to when he spoke of having on the breastplate of righteousness. In a secondary sense, the breastplate of righteousness could refer to the practicing of righteousness. Holy living makes it a little more difficult for the devil to lay a guilt trip on us.

Boots of Peace

We are to have our feet shod with the preparation of the gospel of peace. The Roman soldier wore a studded sandal in battle that gave him security and helped him stand immovable in the conflict. Those shoes gave him confidence. He had peace in the midst of warfare. The peace of God gives us security and confidence in battle. It's the peace of God that protects us from discouragement and despair.

Shield of Faith

We come now to the shield of faith. The particular shield referred to here was a large one that the soldier could hide completely behind. This shield would thoroughly protect him from the barrage of arrows sent by the enemy. What this shield did for the Roman soldier, the shield of faith does for the Christian. The shield of faith is an active trust in the nature, character, love, and promises of God that are all made known to us through His Word. This shield shelters us from the flaming arrows of the wicked one.

Helmet of Salvation

The final piece of defensive equipment is the helmet of salvation. This helmet protects our minds from attacks against the assurance of our salvation. Satan will accuse us of not doing enough for God and then will call into question the validity of our salvation. Understanding and applying the doctrine of salvation by grace alone is what it means to put on the helmet of salvation. Again, this knowledge comes through the Scriptures. *"For by grace you have been saved through faith, and that not of yourselves; it is the gift of God, not of works, lest anyone should boast"* (Ephesians 2:8–9). *"Not by works of righteousness which we have done, but according to His mercy He saved us"* (Titus 3:5). To lay hold of these truths is to put on the helmet of salvation.

Sword of the Spirit

We come now to the final piece of the armor and the only offensive weapon. The sword of the Spirit which is the Word of God. "It is that which God has spoken, His Word, the Bible. The Bible is sharper than any two-edged sword. It is the wisdom of God and the power of God. It commends itself to the reason and conscience. It has the power not only of truth but of divine truth. In opposition to all error, to all false philosophy, to all false principles of morality, to all the fallacies of vice, to all the suggestions of the devil, the sole, simple and sufficient answer is the Word of God. The Word of God puts to flight all the powers of darkness.

The power of God's Word is accessible for the individual Christian as well as for the church collectively. All of our triumphs over sin and error are effected by the Word of God. So long as we use the Word of God and rely on it alone, we go on conquering; but when anything else, be it reason, science, tradition, or the commandments of men, is allowed to take its place or to share its office, then the church, or the Christian, is at the mercy of the adversary."

Our Example in Battle

By a brief consideration of the earthly ministry of our Lord we can see how the sword of the Spirit is used. We've already considered the confrontation between Christ and Satan in the wilderness and seen how Jesus put Satan to flight with the Word of God. We find the same occurrence again and again throughout our

Lord's ministry as He dealt with the scribes and the Pharisees.

On each occasion our Lord's skillful use of the sword of the Spirit silenced His enemies. Take for example the situation recorded in Matthew 21:15 and 16. The religious leaders were angry with Jesus for allowing the children to refer to Him as the Messiah. Do you remember His response? *"Have you never read, 'Out of the babes and nursing infants You have perfected praise'?"*

How about the time when the Sadducees posed to Him a hypothetical situation that they thought to be an air-tight argument against the resurrection. His response was *"your mistake is not knowing the Scriptures or the power of God,"* and again He said, *"have you not read what was spoken to you by God?"* (Matt. 22:29,31). One last example is found in the Lord's response to the Pharisee's assertion that Christ was to be merely the son of David, *"How can they say that Christ is the son of David? Now David himself said in the Book of Psalms"* (Luke 20:41–44). In each of these examples we are being taught indirectly by the Captain of our salvation how to effectively wield the sword of the Spirit.

Now that we have defined the armor of

God, we need to consider what it means to put it on. For the exhortation is to "put on the whole armor of God." Since the armor of God is an understanding and application of the Word of God, putting on the armor of God refers then to being equipped with a thorough knowledge of the Scriptures. Our knowledge of the Scriptures will increase as we spend time reading, meditating, studying, and memorizing them. Let me give you a quick overview of each of these different approaches to the Word.

Reading

Reading is our first and most simple approach to the Scriptures. Perhaps we begin in Genesis and go right through to Revelation. On our way the Holy Spirit is slowly, but surely reprogramming us and creating in us a Christ-centered world view. By consistently reading through the Scriptures we are being trained by the Holy Spirit to think spiritually. The Lord is imparting to us the mind of Christ. I like to read my Bible in the evenings before going off to sleep. It's a great way to end the day. By reading at average speed for forty-five minutes to an hour each evening, we can get through the entire Bible in less than a year. Once you've finished, go back to Genesis and start all over again. The better we know the written Word, the better we'll know the living Word; the Lord Jesus Christ.

Meditation

Meditation is our next approach to the Scriptures. Meditation of course includes reading, but goes much deeper than that. The word *meditate* means to ponder. It means to talk to oneself. That's what we're to do with the Word. We're to think about it. We're to talk to ourselves about it. We're to talk to the Lord about it.

Meditating differs from reading because it takes more time and greater concentration. When meditating on a portion of Scripture, I'm praying over it and at the same time asking myself questions. To whom was this written? What does it say? How does it apply to me? What are some other Scriptures that relate to what's being said? When meditating, I usually have a pen and note pad handy in order to jot down anything the Lord might say to me during that time. Meditation for me is best early in the morning and from the New Testament. However, each of us have to find our own niche.

So find the time that is best for you. The promise of blessing is to the one *"whose delight is in the Law of the Lord, and in His law, he does meditate day and night"* (Psalm 1:2). Try to spend as much time as you can meditating on the Word. Make it a priority!

Study

Studying the Bible is something that every Christian needs to learn to do. The difference between reading and meditating on the Word and studying the Word would be the use of certain study helps or tools. By tools I mean things like: concordances, Bible dictionaries, Bible handbooks, Greek and Hebrew word studies, commentaries, etc. All of these can be very helpful in our understanding of the Scriptures. If for some reason these types of resources are not available to you, a good study Bible will do.

Another way of fulfilling the need for Bible study is to sit under an anointed Bible teacher who teaches systematically through the Scriptures. If you have this somewhat rare opportunity, I exhort you to thank God and take full advantage of it. In whatever way is best for you, make Bible study a regular part of your life and know that in doing so you're further equipping yourself with the armor of God.

Memorization

My final word in relation to putting on the whole armor of God is Scripture memorization. Committing the Word of God to memory is indeed a vital part of putting on the whole armor of God. In John's first epistle, chapter 2 verse 14 he states that the strength of the young men and their victory over the devil was the result of the Word of God abiding in them. There's no better way to assure the Word of God is abiding in you than by memorizing it.

Start by reading over and over again those Scriptures that speak most powerfully to you. If need be, write them down on a piece of paper and read them several times over each day until they become part of you. You'll find that those particular verses will be powerful resources in your overall arsenal of spiritual weapons.

Finally, remember this is God's armor and, therefore, we can be assured that as we take it up the victory is ours. The question that remains is: Will we take it up? God help us to do so, for our spiritual well-being depends on it.

Chapter 6

Fit for the Fight

Praying always with all prayer and supplication in the Spirit, being watchful to this end with all perseverance and supplication for all the saints.

Ephesians 6:18

The Christian soldier now stands fully dressed for battle. However, he is still not ready to fight. He lacks two essential things to victory—skill and strength. Although a soldier may be equipped with the best weapons, if he is without skill and strength, victory is uncertain at best. What physical fitness and mental preparedness are to those fighting in the natural realm, prayer is to the Christian soldier. Prayer is the final piece of the Christian soldier's armor. Prayer is the assurance that the Christian soldier is fit for the fight.

The Scriptures are filled with exhortations to prayer: *"Continue steadfastly in prayer"* (Romans 12:12). *"Continue earnestly in prayer, being vigilant in it with thanksgiving"* (Colossians 4:2). *"Pray without ceasing"* (1 Thessalonians 5:17).

Prayer is vital. It is essential to victory in this spiritual battle. Yet, it is often neglected. The neglect of prayer is one of the main reasons for the weakness of many Christians as well as the weakness of the modern church. Most Christians and churches do everything, but pray! We obviously have failed to understand the importance of prayer. John Bunyan, the author of *Pilgrim's Progress,* and a man who spent thirteen years in prison for preaching the gospel, said: "You can do more than pray after you've prayed, but you cannot do more than pray until you have prayed." Spurgeon said: "My heart has no deeper conviction than this, that prayer is the most efficient spiritual agency in the universe next to the Holy Spirit.... I could as soon think of living without eating or breathing, as living without praying." May God impart to us the same conviction that these men had concerning prayer.

In our text we are told five things about praying in connection with spiritual warfare.

Pray Always

First, we are told to pray always. To "pray always" means that throughout the course of the day, over and over again, we are to lift our hearts in prayer to God, bringing before Him the issues we're facing. John Wesley described the man who fulfills the injunction to "pray without ceasing."

> *His heart is ever lifted up to God at all times and in all places. In this he is never hindered, much less interrupted, by any person or thing. In retirement or company, leisure, business, or conversation his heart is ever with the Lord. Whether he lie down or rise up, God is in all his thoughts. He walks with God continually having the loving eye of his mind still fixed upon Him and everywhere seeing Him that is invisible.*

This is what Paul means when he says to pray always.

Pray in the Spirit

Next we are to pray in the Spirit. This means to be led by the Spirit in prayer. The way to assure we're praying in the Spirit is to ask the Spirit's assistance as we go to prayer. There's nothing quite as wonderful or thrilling as being empowered by the Holy Spirit in prayer. The heart is impassioned. The mind is clear. Every thought is ordered. Praise, petitions, and intercessions flow freely, and one can literally pray for hours and feel that only a few moments have passed. Seek to pray in the Spirit. Spend time asking the Lord to lead before you begin your prayer time. You'll find this kind of prayer to be a great adventure and a great faith builder.

Oswald Sanders, former director of the China Inland Mission, said this in regards to Spirit-led prayer, *"The very fact that God lays a burden of prayer on our hearts and keeps us praying is evidence that He purposes to grant the answer."*

When asked if he really believed that the two men for whom he had prayed for more than fifty years would be converted, George Mueller replied, *"Do you think that God would have kept me praying all these years if He did not intend to save them?"* This is Spirit-led prayer.

Watchful in Prayer

After praying in the Spirit the exhortation is now to be watchful in prayer. Be alert. Be on your guard. Pay attention and be ready always to do battle in prayer. Is the Lord moving? Pray! Is the enemy attacking? Pray! Has a fellow soldier fallen? Pray! Set a vigil! Get a prayer partner! Pray! Pray! Pray!

Perseverance in Prayer

From watchfulness we come to perseverance in prayer. Have you ever prayed about something and felt like no one was listening? Time and time again you've brought your request before the Lord and yet nothing changes? What do you do then? If you're like most people, you'll be tempted to just give up. Don't do that! Jesus spoke a parable with the intention of communicating that men should always pray and not lose heart (Luke 18:2–8).

When we don't see immediate answers to our prayers we tend to want to give up. When we desire to give up, we need perseverance. Effective praying is like running a marathon. Endurance is the key. Do you remember the wonderful promise Jesus made concerning prayer? *"Ask, and it will be given to you; seek, and you will find; knock, and it will be opened to you"* (Matthew 7:7).

What most people fail to realize is that this is a conditional promise. Unfortunately, the condition is missed in most of our English translations. The condition is perseverance. A literal rendering of the Greek text reads: "keep on asking, keep on seeking, keep on knocking." How many times have we failed to receive an answer to our prayer because we've failed to meet the condition of perseverance?

One of our greatest obstacles to perseverance in prayer is the same one faced by the apostles themselves. Jesus said of them, *"The spirit indeed is willing, but the flesh is weak."* To persevere in prayer takes commitment, discipline, and self-sacrifice. I've already mentioned the fact that George Mueller prayed for more than fifty years for the salvation of two men. Can you imagine how many times he must have felt like giving up? But he was committed, and we must also be committed if we expect to see the enemy vanquished, God's work flourish, and souls brought to Christ. Persevere in prayer. *"You who make mention of the Lord, do not keep silent, and give Him no rest till He establishes and till He makes Jerusalem a praise in the earth"* (Isaiah 62:6–7).

Supplication for All the Saints

The final word on prayer is supplication for all the saints. Praying for God's people is a privilege that each of us has. Are you looking for a ministry? Do you desire to serve the Lord, but have yet to discover your calling? Make this your work for the kingdom—pray for the Church.

Pray for your pastor and all pastors who are genuinely seeking to serve the Lord. Pray for the evangelists who are faithfully preaching the gospel of Christ. Pray for those serving the Lord as missionaries. Pray for all of God's servants who are serving the body of Christ in whatever way.

Pray also for God's people who go out daily into the secular world that they would be filled with the Spirit. Pray that they would be the salt of the earth and the light of the world. Pray for the sick and suffering among God's people. You can have a world-wide ministry and never leave your own city limits by making supplication for all the saints.

Too many people underestimate the power of prayer. God uses the prayers of ordinary people in their own homes to vitally effect and bless

His ministries. A wonderful example of the power of prayer is evidenced in the testimony of Hudson Taylor, a missionary to China.

> *Some years ago the record of a wonderful work of grace in connection with one of the stations of the China Inland Mission attracted a good deal of attention. Both the number and spiritual character of the converts had been far greater than at other stations where the consecration of the missionaries had been just as great. This rich harvest of souls remained a mystery until Hudson Taylor, on a visit to England, discovered the secret. At the close of one of his addresses a gentleman came forward to make his acquaintance. In the conversation which followed, Mr. Taylor was surprised at the accurate knowledge the man possessed concerning the China Inland Mission station. "But how is it," Mr. Taylor asked, "That you are so conversant with the conditions of that work?" "Oh!" He replied, "the missionary there and I are old college mates: for years we have regularly corresponded; he has sent me names of inquirers and converts and these I have daily taken to God in prayer." At last the secret was found— a praying man, praying definitely, praying daily.*

Prayer is the great spiritual exercise that makes one "fit for the fight."

Epilogue

Paul in writing to the Corinthians said that he was not ignorant of Satan's devices (2 Corinthians 2:11). We also are not to be ignorant of Satan's devices. This book has been written with the intent of not only revealing our enemy's character and devices but also of appropriating the victory that God has given us over him. Therefore, Satan's kingdom has been considered as well as his activity in the world and his assault upon God's people. Although he is crafty, intelligent and well-armed, he is powerless against a Christian standing in the whole armor of God and spiritually fit through prayer. The necessity now is to apply what we've learned to our daily walk of faith. The spiritual principles from God's Word can only be applied and practiced through the power of the Holy Spirit. Ask God to fill you with His Spirit and to lead you on to victory. You can be sure He will. "Finally, my brethren, be strong in the Lord and in the power of His might."

How to Become a Christian

First of all you must recognize that you are a sinner. Realize that you have missed the mark. This is true of each of us. We have deliberately crossed the line not once, but many times. The Bible says, *"All have sinned and fallen short of the glory of God"* (Romans 3:23). This is a hard admission for many to make, but if we are not willing to hear the bad news, we cannot appreciate and respond to the *good news*.

Second, we must realize that Jesus Christ died on the cross for us. Because of sin, God had to take drastic measures to reach us. So He came to this earth and walked here as a man. But Jesus was more than just a good man. He was the God-man—God incarnate—and that is why His death on the cross is so significant.

At the cross, God Himself—in the person of Jesus Christ—took our place and bore our sins. He paid for them and purchased our redemption.

Third, we must repent of our sin. God has commanded men everywhere to repent. Acts 3:19 states, *"Repent therefore and be converted, that your sins may be blotted out, so that times of refreshing may come from the presence of the Lord."* What does this word repent mean? It means to change direction–to hang a U-turn on the road of life. It means to stop living the kind of life we led previously and start living the kind of life outlined in the pages of the Bible. Now we must change and be willing to make a break with the past.

Fourth, we must receive Jesus Christ into our hearts and lives. Being a Christian is having God

Himself take residence in our lives. John 1:12 tells us, *"But as many as received Him, to them He gave the right to become children of God."* We must receive Him. Jesus said, *"Behold, I stand at the door and knock. If anyone hears My voice and opens the door, I will come in..."* (Revelation 3:20). Each one of us must individually decide to open the door. How do we open it?. Through prayer.

If you have never asked Jesus Christ to come into your life, you can do it right now. Here is a suggested prayer you might even pray.

Lord Jesus, I know that I am a sinner and I am sorry for my sin. I turn and repent of my sins right now. Thank You for dying on the cross for me and paying the price for my sin. Please come into my heart and life right now. Fill me with Your Holy Spirit and help me to be Your disciple. Thank You for forgiving me and coming into my life. Thank You that I am now a child of Yours and that I am going to heaven. In Jesus' name, I pray. Amen.

When you pray that prayer, God will respond. You have made the right decision–the decision that will impact how you spend eternity. Now you will go to heaven, and in the meantime, find peace and the answers to your spiritual questions.

Other books available in this series...

Spiritual Warfare
by Brian Brodersen
Pastor Brian Brodersen of Calvary Chapel Costa Mesa, California brings biblical balance and practical insight to the subject of spiritual warfare.

The Psychologizing of the Faith
by Bob Hoekstra
Pastor Bob Hoekstra of Living in Christ Ministries calls the church to leave the broken cisterns of human wisdom, and to return to the fountain of living water flowing from our wonderful counselor, Jesus Christ.

Practical Christian Living
by Wayne Taylor
Pastor Wayne Taylor of Calvary Fellowship in Seattle, Washington takes us through a study of Romans 12 and 13 showing us what practical Christian living is all about.

Building Godly Character
by Ray Bentley
Pastor Ray Bentley of Maranatha Chapel in San Diego, California takes us through a study in the life of David to show how God builds His character in our individual lives.

Worship and Music Ministry
by Rick Ryan & Dave Newton
Pastor Rick Ryan and Dave Newton of Calvary Chapel Santa Barbara, California give us solid biblical insight into the important subjects of worship and music ministry within the body of Christ.

Overcoming Sin & Enjoying God
by Danny Bond
Pastor Danny Bond of Pacific Hills Church in Aliso Viejo, California shows us, through practical principles, that it is possible to live in victory over sin and have constant fellowship with our loving God.

Answers for the Skeptic
by Scott Richards
Pastor Scott Richards of Calvary Fellowship in Tucson, Arizona shows us what to say when our faith is challenged, and how to answer the skeptic in a way that opens hearts to the love and truth of Jesus Christ.

Effective Prayer Life
by Chuck Smith
Pastor Chuck Smith of Calvary Chapel Costa Mesa, California discusses the principles of prayer, the keys to having a dynamic prayer life, and the victorious results of such a life. It will stir in your heart a desire to "pray without ceasing."

The Afterglow
by Henry Gainey
Pastor Henry Gainey of Calvary Chapel Thomasville, Georgia gives instruction in conducting and understanding the proper use of the gifts of the Holy Spirit in an "Afterglow Service."

Final Curtain
by Chuck Smith
Pastor Chuck Smith of Calvary Chapel Costa Mesa, California provides insight into God's prophetic plan and shows how current events are leading to the time when one climactic battle will usher in eternity.

For ordering information, please contact:
The Word For Today
P.O. Box 8000, Costa Mesa, CA 92628
(800) 272-WORD
Also, visit us on the Internet at:
www.twft.com